POKéMON ™

1001

STICKER BOOK

ORCHARD

HOW TO USE THIS BOOK

The scenes in this book are missing their Pokémon! Can you find the stickers to fill each page? There are also lots of extra stickers of your favourite Pokémon.

ORCHARD BOOKS

First published in Great Britain in 2018 by The Watts Publishing Group

1 3 5 7 9 10 8 6 4 2

A CIP catalogue record for this book is available from the British Library.

ISBN 978 1 40835 473 5

Printed and bound in China

MIX
Paper from responsible sources

FSC
www.fsc.org

FSC® C104740

Orchard Books

An imprint of Hachette Children's Group

Part of The Watts Publishing Group Limited

Carmelite House

50 Victoria Embankment

London EC4Y 0DZ

An Hachette UK Company

www.hachette.co.uk

www.hachettechildrens.co.uk

THIS BOOK BELONGS TO

_____

Welcome to Kanto! The first partner Pokémon and their evolutions are in the city. Can you find them all on the sticker pages?

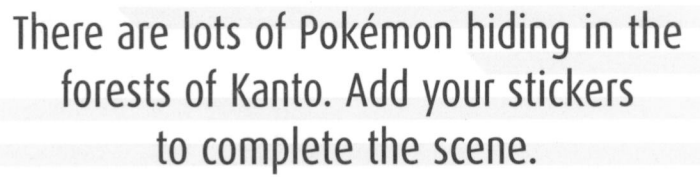

There are lots of Pokémon hiding in the forests of Kanto. Add your stickers to complete the scene.

The Pokémon of Kanto are ready for battle!
Add your stickers to find out who will win.

Pokémon can be found in all sorts of landscapes. Add the Johto first partner Pokémon in the mountains.

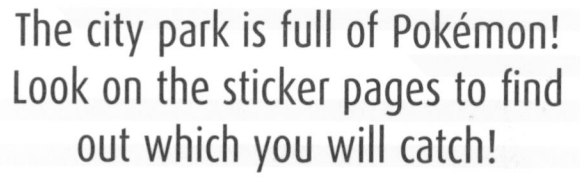

The city park is full of Pokémon!
Look on the sticker pages to find
out which you will catch!

An epic battle is about to begin.
Add the competitors to complete
the exciting scene.

Pokémon have gathered in front of this cave. Can you find the Hoenn first partners, their evolutions and Pikachu?

The volcano on Hoenn has started to smoke. What type of Pokémon have gathered to watch?

Get ready for battle! Who in
Hoenn is up for the challenge?
Add your stickers to find out.

First partner Pokémon have fun
in the forests of Sinnoh. Add
them to the scene.

Many types of Pokémon can be found in Sinnoh. Add your favourites to the scene.

Which Pokémon will battle for victory
in Sinnoh? Add your stickers to
start the tournament!

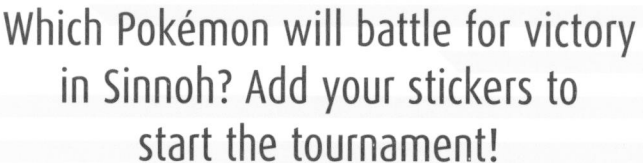

At nighttime in Unova, the first partner evolutions and Pikachu appear from nowhere! Add them to the scene.

Down by the river is a prime spot for
spotting Pokémon in Unova!
Who will you see today?

The battle for Unova has begun!
Add your stickers to complete the scene.

In Kalos, the first partner Pokémon and
their evolutions have gathered together.
Can you add them all to the scene?

Pokémon sometimes gather under the light of the moon! Who has appeared tonight?

The stadium is packed – are you ready
for the ultimate battle? Which
Pokémon will win in Kalos?

The Alolan first partner Pokémon and their evolutions can all be spotted in this scene. Can you find the right stickers?

The beach is packed with Alolan Pokémon.
Which can you spot on the shore?

The stage is set for the final battle in Alola! Who will be victorious?

Pokémon of many types gather by the river. Add your favourite Pokémon to complete this scene.

DON'T MISS THESE OTHER OFFICIAL POKÉMON BOOKS

EARLY READER

Pokémon

ALOLA ADVENTURE

EARLY READER

Pokémon

THE GUARDIAN'S CHALLENGE

EARLY READER

Pokémon

TEAM ROCKET TROUBLE

EARLY READER

Pokémon

BATTLE ON ALOLA

Pokémon

ASH'S BIG CHALLENGE

Pokémon

POKÉMON PERIL

Pokémon

THE ORANGE LEAGUE

Pokémon

SCYTHER VS CHARIZARD

Pokémon

RACE TO DANGER

Pokémon

SHOW TIME!

Pokémon

POWER UP PSYDUCK

Pokémon

THE WINNER'S CUP

Stickers for pages 4-5, 10-11, 16-17, 22-23, 28-29, 34-35, 40-41

Extra stickers